PIERRE F. WALTER

THE AQUARIUS AGE AND
PUBLISHING

A New Paradigm Emerging

"Articles Series"

Published by Sirius-C Media Galaxy LLC

http://sirius-c-publishing.com

http://siriuscmedia.com

http://ipublica.com

ISBN 978-1-468109-93-1

Contact Information Pierre F. Walter

publisher@sirius-c-publishing.com

About Pierre F. Walter

http://drpfw.info

Quotation Suggestion

Pierre F. Walter, *The Aquarius Age and Publishing: A New Paradigm Emerging,* Newark: Sirius-C Media Galaxy LLC, 2011

About the Author

Pierre F. Walter is an author, international lawyer, researcher, corporate trainer, and lecturer. After finalizing studies in German Law, International Law and *European integration* with diplomas obtained in 1981 through 1983, he graduated in December 1987 at the Law Faculty of the University of Geneva as *Docteur en Droit* in international law.

The doctorate was funded by scholarships from the *Swiss Institute of Comparative Law*, Lausanne, and from the *University of Geneva*, as well as a Fulbright Travel Grant for an assistantship with Professor Louis B. Sohn at *UGA Law School Department of International Law*, Athens, Georgia, USA, in 1985. Pierre F. Walter also served as a research assistant to *Freshfields, Bruckhaus, Deringer*, Cologne, Germany in 1983 and to *Lalive Lawyers*, Geneva, in 1987.

Pierre F. Walter writes and lectures in English, German and French languages; he has written *more than ten thousand pages* embracing all literary genres, including *novels, short stories, film scripts, essays, selfhelp books, monographs* and extended *book reviews*. Also a pianist and composer, he has realized 40 CDs with *jazz, newage* and *relaxation music*.

Pierre F. Walter's professional publications span the domains *International Law, Criminal Law, Holistic Science, Psychology, Education, Shamanism, Ecology, Spirituality, Quantum Physics, Systems Theory, Natural Healing, Peace Research, Personal Growth, Selfhelp* and *Consciousness Research*. 110 Book Reviews, thirty-eight audio books and more than hundred video lectures were realized in the years 2005-2010. Besides, Pierre F. Walter is author and editor of *Great Minds Series*, which features scientists, artists and authors of genius from Leonardo to Fritjof Capra.

Pierre F. Walter publishes via his Delaware firm *Sirius-C Media Galaxy LLC* and the imprints IPUBLICA and Sirius-C Media (SCM).

For Nelson

CONTENTS

INTRODUCTION 6

The Aquarius Age and World Peace

Aquarius Age vs. Pisces Age 7

The Aquarius Network Economy 11

The Empowered New Age Citizen 13

THE WEBOLUTION 17

The Future of Publishing

The Fruit of Frustration 18

Self-Publishing 20

Unity.com 27

A Cultural Revolution 42

BIBLIOGRAPHY 47

Contextual Bibliography

FROM THE SAME AUTHOR 65

A Bibliography

INTRODUCTION

The Aquarius Age and World Peace

Aquarius Age vs. Pisces Age

Astrology has predicted the *Aquarius Age* to take its course from about 2000 to 2020; it is the successor of the *Pisces Age*. What does that mean? The Zodiac teaches that life doesn't consist of single isolated events but that all is *interconnected and cyclic*, and therefore subject to repetition and spiraled non-linear evolution. Astrologers have always emphasized the high importance of *cyclical thinking* as opposed to linear thinking. In the evolution of humanity, there are various cycles that describe the characteristics of humanity's phylogenetic development.

These cycles are very long; they do not just embrace years, not just decades, but centuries and millenaries. The most recent of these cycles, that we just left, the *Pisces Age*, lasted approximately two thousand years. The Pisces Age is associated with the 12th House of the Zodiac and thus with the collective, as opposed to the individual, with mass obsessions, and focus on illness instead of health, with secrecy and taboo instead of free speech, and segregation instead of integration. The Ruler of the 12th House is *Neptune* as the ruler of Pisces which symbolizes water and emotions in their raw, non-integrated form.

The *Aquarius Age* is associated with the 11th House of the Zodiac and thus with friendship and brotherhood, with communication beyond borders, and sharing of ideas across cultural boundaries. It is associated with the planet *Uranus* and with the element *air* emphasizing communication as the single most important activity during this cycle.

Let us have a look now at the essential differences in the social and political paradigms that are associated with Pisces Age, on one hand, and Aquarius Age, on the other.

Pisces Age	Aquarius Age
linear, dogmatic, mechanistic thinking	cyclic, functional, systemic thinking
group over individual	power of the individual and groupings
uniformity, dogmatism, tyranny	diversity, democracy, shared power
fundamentalism, absolutism	functionalism
authority and hero worship	self-power
obedience to leaders	obedience to self
mass education, alphabetization	individualized education
mass media, mass manipulation	media on demand, media choices
lack of identity and spirituality	high identity, self-chosen spirituality
lack of autonomy for the young	high autonomy for the young
high cultural uniformity	high cultural diversity
co-dependence, narcissism	emotionally integrated sexuality
locality, provinciality	non-locality, globality, universality
macro-industry	micro-industry
environmental pollution	environmental consciousness
hierarchical and pyramidal structures	flat and neuronal structures
political opacity	political transparence
regional and national values	global values
discarding out, segregating	embracing, integrating
mind-body split	mind-body harmony
accumulation, agglomeration	diversification, recycling
minorities considered as nuisance	minorities considered as enrichment
habitual career choices valued	unusual career choices valued
the neurotic, compulsive character	the genital, flexible character

The general trend under the Aquarius Age will be away from collectivism and toward individualism, away from standard opinions and rules toward more freedom for setting and living our own personalized standards and ways of life.

The regard of the state upon the citizen will largely shift. While within the authoritarian if not totalitarian state of the Pisces Age, the citizen was a *subject*, for the democratic Aquarian state, the citizen is a *customer*. The Aquarius Age shall provide the individual with a greater sphere of self-expression and more options for associating with peers and groupings that pursue similar goals, even if those goals largely differ from the opinions or the life style of the average individual, or the majority.

There will be definitely more space and recognition for alternative life styles. The influence of social and political bodies over the individual will decrease and become more smooth.

Rulership will adopt more of a caretaking nature and a kind of creative partnership with the people under the rule. The leadership paradigm will change from leadership to *stewardship* or servant-leadership, as I have outlined it in my *Idiot Guide to Servant Leadership (2010)*.

In the Pisces Age we see tradition often as a way to justify repression or even tyranny; typically, tradition-holders and tradition-seekers are politically right wing and do all to sabotage the upsurge of a truly pluralistic society. The Aquarian thinker is deeply concerned with reforming and renewing tradition. In Aquarian culture, tradition will be valued as a useful tool for acquiring insights about the human nature, without more. The Aquarius Age will create a society that is highly complex and highly parceled but in which every individual has a much higher chance than before to make out a niche, a viable space and protection as well as social contact in interest circles of the most various kinds.

The Aquarius Network Economy

Regarding the economy, global structural changes will force many traditional businesses to renew themselves for being more flexible and implementing new and integrated solutions. Economies are likely to crash if they are unable to do the structural changes that globalization requires. New ways for financing projects of global dimensions will be found.

It is doubtful that the world economy is going to be maintained on the sole basis of a paper currency such as the dollar; there will probably be a pool of prime currencies that compose, and safeguard, the 'world currency' of the future.

Experts alerted us about the fact that financial conglomerates located mainly in the United States have reached the size of major state budgets. If those large sums of capital are not used wisely, they could jeopardize the world economy.

The danger here is greed-based speculative irresponsibility, which has been systematically bred by the authoritarian and monopolistic social and economic policies of the Pisces Age. Organizations such as the Christian Church, which has been founded under the sign and the symbolism of Pisces, have through their power games manipulated and infantilized the masses to such a degree that the common man is currently not in state to really discern right from wrong or good from bad as far as global policies in economy, justice and social welfare are concerned.

This is so because the information flow today has assumed such gigantic proportions that only professional media experts can channel it and provide daily information that is even remotely accurate. Yet, it is a fact that media multinationals have shown to use their expertise mainly for manipulating information rather than presenting raw information. As a result, the individual, while believing to know more with every coming year, knows actually less of what's really going on in the world. In addition, organized religion and ideologies have all shown their *destructiveness* breeding among human beings separation, segregation, antagonism, arrogance, hatred, jealousy and war.

The transparence typical for the Aquarius Age will gradually disempower the worldwide truth-holder conglomerates and emasculate their imperialistic monopolies and favoritism that enriches an oligarchy beyond all measure, while leaving hundreds of millions mentally, materially and spiritually impoverished! On the other hand, new global business opportunities will arise for those who build on freedom and democracy and who listen to the true needs of the masses. While companies that build on privileges or outmoded traditions, a blown-up self-image or that adhere to undemocratic or even tyrannical forms of leadership will be surprised how quickly and effectively the new era will literally erase them from the surface of international business.

The highest reward will be for those who serve the customer and who have built a service-oriented business model that empowers the consumer, that is transparent, that gives options and that is consistent in structure and constant in time.

The Empowered New Age Citizen

Personal relationships will go new ways in the Aquarius Age. The axis young-old will be emphasized which means there will be less of agism and more communication between the different age segments of society. Relationships and even marriage will be more easily considered okay when partners differ in age. And there will be more rights for children and the youth, also in terms of social outgoingness! Young people will more easily be allowed to move to other places on their own or to engage in relationships with partners of their choice, be it adult sexual mates.

Legal efforts to reform the laws of consent have been considered in all major industrial nations even though not much change has been implemented yet. But the discussion is ongoing. The Aquarius Age will bring the real changes because the present new generation needs to have grown up to implement them. There will be more rights for elders, too, and a more acute awareness about the precious wisdom of elders and the necessity of a socially regulated communication and togetherness of children and elders, as this was realized by Françoise Dolto in the 1980s in Paris, France.[1]

The Aquarian citizen will be more empowered to boycott social collaboration each and every time personal freedom is curtailed down by laws and regulations. This new citizen will more easily become a *social reformer* or even revolu-

---

[1] See Pierre F. Walter, *The Idiot Guide to Sanity (2010)* and Françoise Dolto, *La Cause des Enfants (1985)*.

tionary. This also means that many of the existing forms of social police and denunciation that are undermining personal freedom and trust between people will be abandoned for allowing humanity to develop into a more trustful state of togetherness. It will be seen that peace can only be based upon freedom, trust and abundant soul power of the individual, and not upon ruthless competition, endless hierarchies, oligarchy, tyranny and persecution.

To summarize, the basic peace agenda for the new age could be sketched down in the following slogans:

- lesser social power for the collective;

- more social power for the individual;

- recognition of the child's emotional and sexual completeness;

- abandonment of sex laws and legal focus upon violence;

- retreat of the state to rule human sexuality;

- establishment of emosexual consulting agencies;

- stronger cross-generational and cross-cultural communication;

- more breakthrough power for groupings and social activism;

- civil servants relate to citizens not as subjects but as customers;

- governments behave more and more like traders, businesses;

- government loses absolute jurisdictional immunity;

▸   networked economies;

▸   'pooled' international currency;

▸   help fonds for developing countries taken from that 'pool';

▸   international ecology management and conflict solution;

▸   international arbitrage and peaceful settlement of conflicts.

This list is of course not exhaustive, and when you look at some of the paradigmatic changes involved, you will become aware of the daringness that even today, in the 21st century, such a world peace project entails.[2]

In fact, our mass media do all to prevent world citizens to gain this awareness as our present economies, and their marketing philosophies, are built upon the idea of the 'national state'. However, this monolithic structure is currently eroding more and more with the economic reality of a 'networked' world economy, where national segments are more and more intertwined with each other, and where the entanglement becomes one of global dimensions. It is obvious that the more our national economies are entangled with each other, the lesser are chances that because of national sovereignty conflicts, huge wars will be engaged, simply because the 'winners' and 'losers' can hardly be anticipated, and the danger of 'being hurt' when 'hurting others' becomes a real global concern. It's as if we were all living together today in a

---

[2] See also, Pierre F. Walter, *Toward Social Change, Monograph (2010)*.

huge elevator, and when we begin to shoot around, the danger is not just that we kill each other, but that the elevator will crash down.

THE WEBOLUTION

The Future of Publishing

The Fruit of Frustration

All great inventions have been motivated and initiated by frustration, the frustration about something lacking in our life, the dissatisfaction that an obvious need of many people at a specific point in time was not met. This is true not only for the invention of the light bulb, but for a whole lot of other inventions that belong to our surroundings and improve our daily life and comfort.

The interesting thing about inventions is that they reveal lots about the human nature. When one human being invents, millions of others, who have the same unfulfilled need, just accept that faulty reality. And remain uncreative. It is the one or a handful of people who sense the need and bring about what so many not even dream of.

We can indeed observe historically that human progress was pretty much the merit of individuals, and much less of groups. This is interesting because it goes along with another phenomenon; when you observe a group of people confronted with the same need, you will see that always the majority is either content with what is, the status quo, or although not content with it, unable or anxious to change it. It's always one individual or a handful who dare to be dissatisfied and take action towards change. Therefore we have pioneers. And therefore dissatisfaction is the very seed, and the bliss of progress.

All of you who were at the point to publish and encountered the deep frustrations every writer is confronted with, will understand me when I say that publishing, today more than ever before, is a channeling in the wrong sense. Of course, I am talking about the traditional form of publishing, the one which is done by a publisher, a person or company whose business is the commercial exploitation of sharing. Publishing is sharing, sharing of information or of an aesthetic feeling, sharing of a lifestyle, of experiences. There is a deep ethical foundation in publishing.

Democracy is only thinkable with a continuous flow of information reaching potentially everybody. Publishing also involves the risk to be criticized for one's opinions. It means that publishing requires from the publisher a certain amount of courage.

When Gutenberg printed the Bible, his motivation was probably one of sharing, not in order to make money or a business out of publishing. This is why I suggest that publishing is something directly connected to democracy and at the same time important for the functioning of a democratic society.

Self-Publishing

The Internet began as a computer experiment for some military folks and then developed into a gigantic publishing company. The funny thing about this company is that it has no director and no management team and is self-organized and auto-regulated. Some cynics said once in a while the Web was like a horde of monkeys yelling at each other, and that it therefore had no or very little chance to survive as a serious communication highway.

However, the negativists were, as so often, not heading right with their pessimistic outlook: today the Internet is prospering as an alternative publishing network.

The reasons are obvious. It is the dramatic change in channeling information and the possibility to share all that stuff that can be shared electronically that makes the difference to traditional publishing. It's not really to bring out a book that contains links to other books, as well as voice, image and video content. It's much more like TV having become interactive, before TV really has become interactive. We don't have interactive TV yet and interactive journalism is still a pilot project. But the Internet is that TV that is interactive, or it *has become* that TV, as I am finalizing this text, in December 2011 – perhaps not so when I wrote the first draft for this paper, more than ten years ago. But the intention, then, was already there. And this intention is strongly motivated by reasons. There are reasons why people want to change certain things, or why they want to change a whole business, a whole industry, and even a whole society. There are very manifest reasons, but these reasons are not material-istic, not greed-related in the first place. This is perhaps not always so, but with the Internet, it's surely the case. The rea-sons are related to personal power and to the ideal of *total communication* between human beings.

And that is new. It's new because formerly we were thinking more locally and less globally, we were much more tightly held by our leaders and our militaries, by our flags and our national myths, and much more tightly held within the borders of our national universes. While now the world has become a village.

We still have national borders, flags, and militaries, of course, but we are going to *change the thinker* behind those things, those institutions, and those daily realities. And this thinker, somewhere somehow, has found out that *he or she is more than a thinker*, and that there is more than thinking. We have found out that it's nicer to share thoughts than to think *more*. We have found out that it's even nicer to share thoughts and art, and music, and this beyond our national borders and our national mentalities. We found that all this has some-where somehow something to do with *love*, and that it's love that is the ultimate motivation of this crazy network that we call the Internet.

And with that new vision, we then look at traditional publishing, and we see the traditional publishing situation is such that creative new ways of publishing *are most of the time obstructed* by the simple fact that the publisher is profit-oriented and wants to make sure that the book is sold. This situation makes it gifted writers sometimes very hard or even impossible to *get through* and find the way to their audience.

There are many stories about books that have been refused again and again and finally ended up for weeks or months on bestseller lists. One famous example is the short story *Zen or the Art of Motorcycle Maintenance* by Robert M. Pirsig, one of the most important books of our times, and which yet was refused by one hundred twenty publishers! One can only admire the persistence of the author who approached the 121st publisher who, however reluctantly, accepted publishing. This book rapidly sold as world bestseller and was translated in I don't know how many languages.

My point is that the Internet or, more generally, electronic publishing is a new form of information distribution, and follows different principles than the traditional publishing industry. To publish on the Internet has several major advantages. The Web is *free of the profit filter* built in traditional publishing. A natural selection is made through the interest publications find among users.

The Web is a *living system* which grows naturally and is ruled by more subtle laws and customs than the traditional publishing landscape. These generally unwritten laws are similar to the very foundations of life. This is not astonishing since the Web grew like wild strawberries in the forest, rather than within the boundaries of century-old conventions.

The Web is a landscape where everybody gets a chance to move in, and where everybody who pursues literary interests can learn and grow. And where everybody can build and revise publishing strategies. Okay, you need to channel your stuff, you need to find the right outlet, you need to do your marketing. And when you fail in it you probably will not sell your book. But that is a different pair of shoes compared to the often *senseless rejection encountered time and again with publishing multinationals* because they follow rigid and established success strategies.

It's different because it *feels* different.

I have a friend in Holland who is a psychologist and who has published hundreds of articles and books in several countries and languages, and this within traditional publishing, but he reports that he is helpless in front of the capricious tours played to him by his publishers.

It happened to him several times that his texts were censored or cut down by the editor shortly before publishing, without previous notice. In one case, only by the time that the book was in the store, he had found out about the betrayal. He and several others told me that this was absolutely normal from the side of publishing companies, and worse even if those companies are large and renowned.

Since I was rebellious in this respect, my friends told me that I was never going to publish. They were right and wrong at the same time.

They were right in that *I indeed never published with traditional publishers*, and they were wrong in that *I was going to self-publish my stuff*, and in a way that, when they got to know about it, left them speechless.

My elder friend was always astonished to see me editing my texts on my laptop as if they were the manuscripts of somebody else.

– You waste your time with all this, he used to comment, smiling, since the publisher will disregard it completely and put it in the way *he* likes it.

– *He will not*, used to be my reply. *No publisher ever changed my manuscripts since I never gave any of my manuscripts to a publisher.*

Yet nobody thought at that time of the Web as a real new publishing option that could come even remotely close to traditional publishing.

However, many people still do not grasp that new reality and think the Internet was just an advertising medium. If the Web was only an advertisement tool, it would not have much fascination for authors. Fortunately, all those limited visions of the Web have proven wrong. The world has become unthinkable without online publishing. Today we call it *blog publishing*, but that is surely only one of the many masks that the new media giant is going to wear. First, we were just talking about *home pages*, then we got the *e-book*, then the *blog*, but all these are but peaks of the iceberg of a totally new way of expressing oneself. Because there is not only the word, there is also the image, and there is the film, there is sound and there is music. And all these media can be combined in infinite ways. The industry has really become creative to come up with solutions, and the pace is somewhat too fast, and a lot will be trashed later on because it's all based on trial and error. But why not? That's better than to be based on speculation, or on endless theories and tiresome planning. The market will decide, and that means : all of us – the consumers.

The way we live with art seems to change as a whole in our era of electronic publishing. With the wide use of personal computers, art has eventually become a part of our lives, while before it seemed to be confined within the narrow limits of art galleries and musea.

Of course, at all times there were many more artists on the world than the few who are famous or to be found in *Who is Who* or in VIP lists. Yet with the Internet, the chance that everybody can share his art with many other people, without having to be a VIP are much higher than ever before. It is significant because we use to call local artists all those artists who are not world famous. The attribute *local* we give them means that the circle of people who know them are situated within their local area, such as compound, village, town or region.

With the Web, every artist, without being VIP, has the chance to be more than a local artist since they can be known and appreciated by people around the world. Where information is on the wave, art is on the wave. *Art is but a form of information, perhaps the most elaborated form of it, the most complex one.* And yet its message is often simple. Simplicity in complexity could be a slogan not only for art, but also for the Web. To send a message through the Web today is so simple that a child can do it, but technically seen it is a very complex procedure.

It seems to me that the human intelligence that created the Internet is fundamentally different from all what man has created before that creation. The interesting fact about it is that not one man or woman has created it, but many, often simultaneously cooperating from different points of the globe. The Web was thus perhaps the first really effective global institution we have created.

And that is why, among other reasons that I believe the Internet will grow beyond an information highway to become a political highway as well.

Unity.com

When we compare the Web with another global institution, the United Nations, there are at least two striking differences. The United Nations was a creation of states, at a government level, and not something growing from the base layer of societies. The privileges or advantages that the UN provides were primarily intended for the *principi*, the former kings or rulers, and later for the nation states.

Let's not forget the fact, that for the protection of the individual, international law still provides only a *minimum standard*. Human rights and the rights of minority populations are protected *only within the range of special pacts or agreements*, such as the conventions against torture, yet the nation states are free to join these international agreements, or not.

The second, perhaps more important point of difference is that the United Nations, after their creation, have pretty much split into regional power groups. It's not a coincidence that the European Community was another branch of the same tree, coming out of a vision that people like Woodruff Wilson and, much earlier, even philosophers like Rousseau and Kant had about the future of a united world. At the same time, the European integration was pouring wine into the water of the original idea of a Community of Nations that is truly global.[3]

Therefore, the Web is after all an extraordinary creation, because it has a far-reaching political potential. It is as if it

---

[3] See Pierre F. Walter, *The Idiot Guide to World Peace (2010)*.

had been created by an unconscious will, something like a cosmic intention that is beyond mere human perspectives.

When you observe the development of the Web and the fact that really Mr. Everyone and Mrs. Shareware drive it forward to set new cultural and commercial standards, you will be amazed about the power of the individual. This may sound provocative. Yet we face here a mystery that goes beyond all what we have observed hitherto on the globe, something that is like a new gospel, a new power, and a new global village for all. So, to put it clearly, the Internet is the first international organization that really works in the sense of *res publica*, as the old Romans called political matters. And in that sense, as a forum for the public cause, the Internet really is functional. Minorities, for example, be they racial, political or sexual, are effectively propagated through the Web. The police laws of most countries can prohibit minorities from gathering as long as those gatherings take place within local boundaries. But the police cannot legally control them when these gatherings take place online. Since Web meetings are virtual, they do not fall within those laws.

As a result it can be said that the Web created more democracy and freedom of speech. However, this freedom also means that we have to use it responsibly. If we allow people to abuse of it, we jeopardize our newly gained privilege.

International fundamentalism, secret intelligence services, right-wing movements, misguided groupings and a large mass of frustrated individuals only wait for the chance to exert a tight control over the Web so as to install new and hitherto unknown forms of totalitarian government and rulership.

The only effective way to prevent this from happening is that we exert self-control in all forms of online publishing and virtual communication. This implies that we have to become conscious of the value that is linked to freedom and to simple and unprejudiced human communication.

Instead, people seem to ask for more regulation and strict guidelines for conduct on the virtual space. This is totally within the old paradigm. It means to restrict freedom again because a certain amount of frivolous people are unable to use it responsibly. If we want to avoid this result, we have only one choice, either to provide organizations with set regulations inviting people to become members for set purposes and to limit communication to set purposes and for set interests or topics – or to *change the paradigm.*

What is presently taking place on the Web is the first alternative. It means basically to create cages for people who have not learned to conduct themselves properly outside of those cages, in freedom. Human history was an up and down of times of more and less freedom. But at all times certain people searched for cages because they were afraid of freedom or abused of it to the detriment of all. However, it's not that difficult to live in wild life.

First of all, the Web, at its beginnings, grew rather wildly into what it is today. And this is rather a positive circumstance in my opinion because, compared to traditional forms of communication, the Web invites users to become spontaneously creative. Furthermore, if we respect ourselves and others from a basic inner attitude that forms part of a new paradigm in human togetherness, *we do not need organizations that restrict our freedom*, nor rules of conduct. Because we will innately engage in the right and convenient forms of behavior for our largely enhanced ways and forms of communication.

Sounds like Utopia? Let's see now together what implications both paradigms, the old and the new, have for our further human evolution in general, and the evolution of the Web, in particular.

The *old paradigm* represents a system of beliefs that goes from a premise that humans are *basically enemy to each other* and therefore use deceiving means and strategies in order to communicate.

Typical for the old paradigm is a range of prejudice and *phantom beliefs* among people belonging to an in-group, regarding those belonging to an out-group. All those beliefs render communication ineffective and, in extreme cases, impossible. We should always keep in mind that war among humans is only possible from the moment communication has stopped or has been undermined by phantom beliefs and superstitions. The old paradigm is deeply conditioned by the *scarcity mentality*, the belief that nature provides only for a certain number of individuals leaving deprived all others. Despite the fact that everybody who has observed nature clearly sees that one of the basic patterns of nature is abundance, and not scarcity, the adepts of the scarcity principle mentality continue to plague the rest of humanity with their negativism, thus being responsible for the perpetuation of the old paradigm.

These people are easy to recognize; they typically argue for *protection, guidance and security* when asked for engaging in communication with others, be it in virtual space or in real life. They consider all people as *strangers* who have not qualified to be friends, associates or at least acquaintances. The qualification of a person as a stranger means that the person is *potentially dangerous*.

The underlying belief these people share is that the world was a hostile battlefield of conflicting interests and desires, probably simply because their own inner life represents such a battlefield of conflicting interests and desires and they have never found a way to experience inner peace.

These people tend to believe in *Darwinism* in its most destructive dimension, seeing in all human competition an element of the survival of the fittest. As a result of their conditioning and their dominant belief system, the adepts of the old paradigm maintain *virtual and real borders and frontiers* in the world, intelligence services, armies and other destruction devices because their main defense mechanism is aggression. In order to communicate, the adepts of the old paradigm *gather within set organizations for set purposes*, subscribing to set rules of behavior that fundamentally restrict their freedom.

They justify their sacrifice of freedom with their pretended gain in social and political security through the *big brothers* they have created. Unaware of the illusion they are victim of, they strive to give more and more power to those big brothers, thus jeopardizing in the long run the human condition, and even our survival as a human race.

The *new paradigm* represents a system of beliefs which basically admits that humans are made to be *friends and brothers* to each other. Adepts of the new paradigm question why humans react aggressively or with hostility to everything new or unknown, and tend to be more open and communicative in situations that provide doors to the unknown.

Typical for the new paradigm in communication is the attitude to *potentially welcome every possible new encounter*, be it with representatives or forces opposite to one's own culture or conditioning, thus considering unforeseen experiences as challenges and chances for growth and evolution. Adepts of the new paradigm can be recognized because of their *courage, curiosity, openness and a generally adventurous spirit* which considers every human interaction at its root as a great potential chance for love, harmony, understanding and mutual help. It is the adepts of the new paradigm who have created the wonderful new jungle that we today call the Internet, although at the present moment the representatives of the old paradigm *seem to dominate* its general landscape.

Adepts of the new paradigm question the necessity of joining large organizations in order to maintain power within the collective. They value the individual to such extent that they tend to *generally question the institution of organizations that regulate and channel human encounters* thus demonstrating more trust for spontaneous human relations within an unorganized gray area of human interaction.

Adepts of the new paradigm therefore are more *open to unusual or unforeseen aspects of human relations*, be they on an intellectual, psychological, artistic or sexual level. In my opinion, the most important trait of adherents of the new paradigm is their *general openness to restructure human relations* in accordance with all lessons we have collectively learned from the past, with the ultimate goal to enhance human happiness and welfare, personal and societal prosperity and quality of life in the future. Adherents of the new paradigm are generally grateful for new possibilities of human interaction and they tend to value the Web as a *precious new tool and adventure* that has its major advantage not on a commercial or economical, but on a purely human level.

For these reasons the adepts of the new paradigm are usually very busy learning, using and teaching all the features the Web offers us for creating new forms of human interaction and exchange. Among them are the geniuses who treasure the holy grail of the Web, the highest vision about the Web as one of the most important features of life in future centuries. Although constantly exposed to criticism and typical modern-day skepticism, these people build on the positive image they maintain about life, themselves, others and humankind and thus help us all to create the foundations of a better world.

On the Web, presently, the adherents of the new paradigm represent a *small minority of intellectuals* who are, unfortunately, not yet really organized. They tend to fight single and isolated wars within the fields of their specific interests and occupations. One of the reasons they actively engage in publishing and providing publishing opportunities to others on the Web, on a purely non-profit basis, is that they set out to practically realize their high humanitarian vision of the Web. However, without doubt it is the adepts of the new paradigm who are actively involved in the further evolution of the Web and new forms of media such as interactive TV, and developing high-level *edutainment* for large masses of people who seek their personal evolution outside of set organizations and ideologies.

Another important aspect of the revolution that the Web presently undergoes is the profound change that it brings about within and between our *economies*. It cannot be denied that human progress has also an important material dimension. Those who, like me, have lived for years in so-called developing countries know how fundamental for personal evolution it is to have access to educational, and this means today technological, assets. It has become obvious that there cannot be a future culture without technology or based upon an outmoded technology that is mechanistic and inhuman. Technology transfer becomes demonic in the moment it is used as a pretext for getting rid of life-destroying technologies that witness our greatest errors of the past.

The Web has changed traditional economic rules or, for the least, offers an alternative economic concept for its users. Parallel to the development of the Web the software production technology has created the *shareware concept* as a new, hitherto unknown way to provide the use of products against later, and in practice voluntary, payment.

This is really new because traditionally contracts on the purchase of goods legally require the payment of the price after product has moved. Later payment is considered as a form of credit and as such not immediately covered by the contract. Legally, the credit agreement would be considered as a second contract, apart from the original purchase contract, and different in nature from the latter.

The new and revolutionary difference in the shareware concept is its inherent trust in the user's willingness or readiness to pay the requested price, by registering the software. In practice, we all know that *many people never ever register* a large part of shareware programs they operate. But this is exactly part of the system. It's a really human system because it does not discard out the factor of human imperfection, but in the contrary calculates this factor, as it were, in the final bill. This is why the shareware concept, while a few decades ago it would have been considered a totally mad idea, makes sense and works; many a programmer although not becoming a millionaire, can make a modest living out of sales engendered by shareware distribution. That shareware works, two requirements must be met:

▸ The software must be useful and work without major bugs;

▸ The software must be distributed large-scale.

The Web has come at the right moment for shareware to make it as a new economic concept. Without the global distribution possibilities that it ensures, shareware would be lacking out on the second condition and, as a result, would have disappeared to this day.

In addition to the shareware concept which has implemented a new important modification of the traditional idea of selling products, the Web has brought about a much more careful and concerned general attitude towards the customer, especially in the form of –

- more added value;

- more products for free trial;

- more (accurate) product information;

- more customer service;

- more after-sales service;

- more innovative sales and payment techniques;

- more transparency about the seller;

- more concern about the satisfaction of the buyer.

After all, an online customer is not someone who leaves the shop and disappears. He'll be around, as it were, all the time. Consequently, companies tend to care more about their Web customers and the reputation they can gradually build as reliable and serviceable producers or service givers.

After all, *the online customer can give immediate feedback* by means of e-mail, and will *not hesitate to flame* if he has been tricked out, whereas in *real life*, the willingness or readiness of customers for complaining about insufficient quality or bad price-quality relationship largely depends on the manufacturer's or service provider's attitude. He can be either open to customer feedback or rather put nasty customers off through intransigent and sometimes bluntly dishonest employees who simply insist on denying or refusing the complaining customer's allegations.

Now, if a company would use a similar approach for online customers, it would risk to have its practices very quickly unveiled and publicized on the Web, and thus exposed to a potential billion of people. No reasonable company in the world would bear that risk, which is one of the reasons why purchasing online offers a multitude of privileges and advantages for the end customer.

After all, traditional sales also have improved through the Web because *flaming can be practiced also when people bought their stuff through traditional sales channels*. It's always possible to write about bad experiences with companies in blogs or post them on forums.

Now, let's shift our perspective from the economical to the political and have a closer look at that daring idea of the Web becoming, perhaps not too far in the future, a *real international organization and political forum* of all peoples in the world. We know from the development of the European Union (EU) that the political union is very difficult to realize, and in fact the EU is far from being a political union with all what this would involve for its member states. Probably because so much trust is involved in agreeing about the implementation of new systems of government or to concede national powers to a supranational organism.

The United Nations is another example. They were from the beginning set out to implement a political unification with, in the future, ideally, a *world government.* However, the anxieties were and are so high that the courageous goals were pursued less than half-heartedly. The end result was that *bad compromises were made*, compromises that really were compromising the whole idea and led to an absurd reality which counts as its major fact the *largest bureaucracy in the world*, engendering an irresponsible waste of resources.

But let us ask: where is the Web heading? You may object that it is too far-fetched to admit that the Web could eventually bring about what both the EU and the UN did not achieve: a world community, a union of nations, of peoples. How can? If we take a closer look at this seemingly Utopian idea, we see that there is a fundamental difference between the EU and the UN, on one hand, and the Web, on the other in their respective ways to realize this global union of peoples. The difference is that the Web *begins at the basis* whereas all other present *supranational* or *international* organizations began at the top.

What do I mean? On the Web, masses of people from different cultures get into communicating with each other, first for research or academic purposes, then also for business, the exchange of goods and services, and eventually for simply getting to know each other, looking at one another's home pages, learning from each other, communicating basic needs, feelings and opinions. The trend is that the Web becomes every day more a meeting place for a large variety of people communicating for a large variety of purposes. While in the beginning the user had to write out every single command, with the graphic interface of the *World Wide Web* things became really simple and intuitive. Soon illiterate people will be able to write: they'll just talk and the computer will write for them.

I already pointed out that existing organizations such as the EU and the UN, despite the fact that they were instituted to unify peoples, have begun their work with the top classes of society : the rulers, kings and later the sovereign states, and not really six billion individuals.

If we build a house from the roof, forgetting about its foundation, its basis, the house will crash before it is ready. This is the true reason why neither the EU nor the UN accomplish in reality what they have been created for. *It's because they were established as roof structures that lack the foundation.* They came about through governmental collaboration and agreements, and not as a result of the will and the work of the people who have set these governments in place. They have not grown from the base layer of society, but from its top range.

That is why I am convinced that the Web will be the foundation for the true union of peoples in not too distant a future. The Web grew without any governmental control, although it was, paradoxically, created for governmental purposes. Yet from the moment it was given to the public by the American military agencies that had created it, it was a free landscape for new discoveries. And it quickly grew beyond national borders and cultures.

My idea may seem uncanny. Consider that also on the national level, stability was reached only from the moment that the peoples themselves chose their governments. This is not so much a function of the *constitutional system* which can be *monarchic* or *republican*. As long as a king or ruler is firmly based upon the trust of his people, his government will bring about effective solutions and bear fruits. Some of the old Chinese kings who founded their rulership upon the true interest of their people and universal laws have given abundant evidence to this historical and political fact.

On the other hand, the best republican government that is corrupt and has lost the confidence of the majority of citizens, will disappear sooner or later and leave a vacuum of frustration and a bad taste in the mouth of the populace.

What is decisive only is that the system is *truly democratic*. On the national as well as the international level, democracy brings about stability. Governments who do not enjoy the backup of their peoples, reign in unstable conditions and can be thrown over by social unrest and upheaval.

The present international organizations are for the great majority established *from above*, without democratic elections from the side of the peoples. This is one of the reasons why the *man in the street*, be it in the West or the East, when asked about the United Nations or similar organizations, either admits ignorance and gives a negative or indifferent judgment. *Simply because they have not been directly involved in the creation of the organization or the election of its staff.* How can these organizations then seriously attempt to build a future world government? They would reign over people who do not even know them. Therefore, if these organizations, as it seems now, are unable to allow reforms, they will disappear.

This is in part also valid for the EU. However, in the government of the EU, there is much more consciousness about the need for a democratic setup than, for example, in the United Nations. That is why a few years ago the European Parliament has been fundamentally reformed and direct elections for the European parliamentarians have been institutionalized. In the public opinion all over Europe this step was considered uniformly as an advancement of the unification progress, although skepticism prevailed as to how the EU will practically carry out the will of the peoples at its basis, and not only the will of their governments or top-class industrials.

The Web has grown from the root up, and not from the branches down, as all present political international organizations did. Therefore, the chance that my prediction will come true is, I think, higher than the chance that it will not. For it is much easier and much more effective to learn a healthy body perform more functions than to teach a sick and dysfunctional body to perform even very few basic functions. And the present international organizations are not only *sick and dysfunctional*, they waste human and financial resources to such an extent that their maintenance equals ruin for all those who, willingly or unwillingly, have to finance them. And that is all of us.

A Cultural Revolution

Just as the book, once it appeared after the invention of printing, revolutionized the world and our lifestyle, *the e-book gave us another revolution*. Not only because the e-book is read not on paper, but onscreen, but because this kind of book is a *multimedia book*. The fantasy of the reader will not be left on its own, as before, but *actively stimulated by multimedia links* such as photos, videos and interactive functions. From here, to *combine authoring with embedding virtual reality* in order to create the photorealistic picture of an artificial, artistically created world, is but a tiny step.

Visions are a non-touchable reality. Not only that they create reality and are the necessary predecessors of any creation, *vision is by itself a form of reality*. A vision is not a tool only, it is a form of being, not a seed only, but a fully grown tree. Visions form an invisible reality behind the visible one. They directly tap into what Aristotle called *eidos* and Plato *ideas*. You could imagine this world of vision which is universal, as a second reality, another virtual reality that is hidden for our senses yet real for our mind, our non-sensory perception and our imagination. The visualization of new reality is not only a creative game, but creation in itself. *This is a subtle difference.* Many people grasp well that imagination has creative power, yet only a few will admit that imagination represents a world in itself, *another reality which is already existent*, or existential, and *not only a potentiality* for the creation of future existential reality.

Human creation is basically built upon visions. Visions are at the origin of all human progress. The word vision originally means *sight*. We see into the future, or into a better reality, with our inner eye. And we *foresee* events or things *before the time is ripe for them* or the technological standard is existent to produce them in our tangible reality. Our inner visions are situated outside the time-space continuum. They are part of *universal intelligence* which precedes the time-bound, earth-bound continuum and which is eternal.

Publishing is for a great part sharing inner visions. Once this process was not a global one, but locally very limited. One shared with neighbor villagers, the extended family, the clan. Today it may happen to you, especially if you live in a big town, that you share your visions after breakfast with people from another continent via the Web, whereas you have not even said hello to your neighbor for the last two months. The fact is today that the people we are sharing with may live on the other side of the globe. It's not as folk wisdom says that the good is always in front of your eyes or at the entry of your door. That was true long ago and it may be true in other respects. As far as communication and the sharing of experience is concerned, it is *not easy to find friends among your neighbors* if you are not member of the local football club and do not hang around in the local beer bar or coffee house. Let's say your interests are Balinese Gamelan music and Renaissance literature, your favorite artist Dali, your films the old Charlie Chaplin movies, and your passion child photography, *with whom within a radius of ten miles around can you share your interests?*

Our age is one of uniformity, of vulgarity and frivolity, of common standards in almost all areas of life; yet it is paradoxically at the same time one of *individuality and marginality* who find their place in small groups that are wired with each other by the fine cords of telephone lines and that hang out at different times since group members live in different time zones. On the Web, you can hang out anytime you wish since your server serves twenty-four hours, and mailboxes patiently wait until you retrieve their content. While you are logged in, the other members of your little interest group may sleep, fact which by no means impedes your new network friendships from blossoming.

Publishing on the Web means to expose your book or multimedia product to an *unlimited audience*. Bill Gates wrote in *The Road Ahead (1995)* about devices to come on the world market that are small electronic books which we purchase ordinarily, and which have the advantage to provide not only text but the whole range of multimedia built in them.

By now, this idea is already realized, yet I can't see the revolution in that. The difference, in my opinion, of the new information age compared to the old age is not so much the form of the information, *but the way this information is distributed*. Until now, it seems that the Web is understood by most people as a provider of information, a shopping mall, an efficient research tool, an advertising forum and a new way of private and professional communication. The perspective that the Web *could once completely replace our school system* is perhaps far-fetched regarding the reluctance of most governments to invest more than the strict minimum into the reformation and progression of our educational systems. Here we are confronted with an actual change of consciousness.

In the meantime, the number of basic and secondary schools that have their web page grows quickly. If children learn at an early age how to manage Internet access and communicate properly with a large range of people, they have little to learn later on once confronted with team-integration and communication at the workplace or in a business of their own. Our children grow into the information age and many, before they touch the keyboard of a PC, know to manage their game boys and video games. Since the logic and often the handling of electronic devices are similar, our children *will very soon be our masters and teachers, and more, our consultants* in all what concerns the essential bones of the global information network.

Common sense and practical reasons speak for a strong implication of the *next generations* into the actual growth process of the Internet. If our governments do not care about a transformation of the educational systems, *private institutions will and a growing number of parents shall send their children to alternative schooling*.

Children sitting through their most learn-intensive age on 19th century school benches with no access to technology are educated towards being either slaves or cultural cripples in the near future. Those children will have to learn later on, with more effort and perhaps less pleasure what they could have learned by playing in their early age. We are confronted with the fact daily. People loose their jobs because of the restructuring of the global industrial network, the different use and availability of resources, changing technologies and life-styles, and a rapidly growing turn from a *nation-centered economy* to an international one. This makes for a large number of people worldwide who are in transition from job to job, and from place to place. Some never understand that in our times, we have to learn constantly. Those remain jobless. Others *learn to learn and to relearn*; they are flexible or have learned to be flexible.

They will find new, and perhaps more fulfilling jobs or realization opportunities. Some of them become outstanding examples of entrepreneurship, simply because they took a passion for one or the other of the new technologies and put all their energy in a project that changed not only their life, but also their social standard.

BIBLIOGRAPHY

Contextual Bibliography

Abrams, Jeremiah (Ed.)

Reclaiming the Inner Child
New York: Tarcher/Putnam, 1990

Die Befreiung des Inneren Kindes
Die Wiederentdeckung unserer ursprünglichen kreativen Persönlichkeit
und ihre zentrale Bedeutung für unser Erwachsenwerden
München: Scherz Verlag, 1993

Ariès, Philippe

L'enfant et la famille sous l'Ancien Régime
Paris, Seuil, 1975

Centuries of Childhood
New York: Vintage Books, 1962

Geschichte der Kindheit
Frankfurt/M: DTV, 1998

Arntz, William & Chasse, Betsy

What the Bleep Do We Know
20th Century Fox, 2005 (DVD)

Down The Rabbit Hole Quantum Edition
20th Century Fox, 2006 (3 DVD Set)

Bleep
An der Schnittstelle von Spiritualität und Wissenschaft
Verblüffende Erkenntnisse und Anstösse zum Weiterdenken
Berlin: Vak Verlag, 2007

Arroyo, Stephen

Astrology, Karma & Transformation
The Inner Dimensions of the Birth Chart
Sebastopol, CA: CRSC Publications, 1978

Astrologie, Karma und Transformation
Die Chancen schwieriger Aspekte
Frankfurt/M: Heyne Verlag, 1998

Relationships and Life Cycles
Astrological Patterns of Personal Experience
Sebastopol, CA: CRCS Publications, 1993

Handbuch der Horoskop–Deutung
Berlin: Rowohlt, 1999

Atlee, Tom
The Tao of Democracy
Using Co–Intelligence to Create a World That Works for All
North Charleston, SC: Imprint Books / WorldWorks Press, 2003

Bandler, Richard
Get the Life You Want
The Secrets to Quick and Lasting Life Change
With Neuro–Linguistic Programming
Deerfield Beach, Fl: HCI, 2008

Barron, Frank X., Montuori, et al. (Eds.)
Creators on Creating
Awakening and Cultivating the Imaginative Mind
(New Consciousness Reader)
New York: P. Tarcher/Putnam, 1997

Boldt, Laurence G.
Zen and the Art of Making a Living
A Practical Guide to Creative Career Design
New York: Penguin Arkana, 1993

How to Find the Work You Love
New York: Penguin Arkana, 1996

Zen Soup
Tasty Morsels of Zen Wisdom From Great Minds East & West
New York: Penguin Arkana, 1997

The Tao of Abundance
Eight Ancient Principles For Abundant Living
New York: Penguin Arkana, 1999

Das Tao der Fülle
Vom Reichtum, der uns glücklich macht
Mittelberg: Joy Verlag, 2001

Branden, Nathaniel

How to Raise Your Self-Esteem
New York: Bantam, 1987

Die 6 Säulen des Selbstwertgefühls
Erfolgreich und zufrieden durch ein starkes Selbst
München: Piper Verlag, 2009

Butler-Bowden, Tom

50 Success Classics
Winning Wisdom for Work & Life From 50 Landmark Books
London: Nicholas Brealey Publishing, 2004

50 Klassiker des Erfolgs
Die wichtigsten Werke von Kenneth Blanchard, Warren Buffet,
Andrew Carnegie, Stephen R. Covey, Spencer Johnson,
Benjamin Franklin, Napoleon Hill, Nelson Mandela, Anthony Robbins,
Brian Tracy, Sun Tsu, Jack Welch und vielen anderen
Frankfurt/M: MVG Verlag, 2005

50 Lebenshilfe Klassiker
Frankfurt/M: MVG Verlag, 2004

50 Klassiker der Psychologie
Die wichtigsten Werke von Alfred Adler, Sigmund Freud,
Daniel Goleman, Karen Horney, William James, C.G. Jung, Jean Piaget,
Viktor Frankl, Howard Gardner, Alfred Kinsey, Abraham Maslow, Iwan
Pawlow, Stanley Milgram, Martin Seligman und vielen anderen
Frankfurt/M: MVG Verlag, 2004

50 Klassiker der Spiritualität
Die wichtigsten Werke von Augustinus, Khalil Gibran, Mahatma Ghandi,
Dag Hammarskjölkd, Hermann Hesse, C. G. Jung, Eckhart Tolle,
J. Krishnamurti, Thich Nhat Hanh, Mutter Teresa, Dan Millman
und vielen anderen
Frankfurt/M: MVG Verlag, 2006

Chopra, Deepak

Creating Affluence
The A-to-Z Steps to a Richer Life
New York: Amber-Allen Publishing (2003)

Synchrodestiny
Discover the Power of Meaningful Coincidence to Manifest Abundance
Audio Book / CD
Niles, IL: Nightingale-Conant, 2006

The Seven Spiritual Laws of Success
A Practical Guide to the Fulfillment of Your Dreams
Audio Book / CD
New York: Amber-Allen Publishing (2002)

Die Sieben Geistigen Gesetze des Erfolgs
Berlin: Ullstein Verlag, 2004

The Spontaneous Fulfillment of Desire
Harnessing the Infinite Power of Coincidence
New York: Random House Audio, 2003

Covey, Stephen R.

The 7 Habits of Highly Effective People
Powerful Lessons in Personal Change
New York: Free Press, 2004
15th Anniversary Edition
First Published in 1989

Die 7 Wege zur Effektivität
Prinzipien für persönlichen und beruflichen Erfolg
Offenbach: Gabal Verlag, 2009

The 8th Habit
From Effectiveness to Greatness
London: Simon & Schuster, 2004

Der 8. Weg
Von der Effektivität zur wahren Grösse
Offenbach: Gabal Verlag, 2006

De Bono, Edward

The Use of Lateral Thinking
New York: Penguin, 1967

The Mechanism of Mind
New York: Penguin, 1969

Sur/Petition
London: HarperCollins, 1993

Tactics
London: HarperCollins, 1993
First published in 1985

Taktiken und Strategien erfolgreicher Menschen
Frankfurt/M: MVG Verlag, 1995

Serious Creativity
Using the Power of Lateral Thinking to Create New Ideas
London: HarperCollins, 1996

DiCarlo, Russell E. (Ed.)

Towards A New World View
Conversations at the Leading Edge
Erie, PA: Epic Publishing, 1996

Dürckheim, Karlfried Graf

Hara: The Vital Center of Man
Rochester: Inner Traditions, 2004

Hara
Die Erdmitte des Menschen
Neuausgabe
München: O.W. Barth bei Scherz, 2005

Zen and Us
New York: Penguin Arkana 1991

The Call for the Master
New York: Penguin Books, 1993

Absolute Living
The Otherworldly in the World and the Path to Maturity
New York: Penguin Arkana, 1992

The Way of Transformation
Daily Life as a Spiritual Exercise
London: Allen & Unwin, 1988

Der Alltag als Übung
Vom Weg der Verwandlung
Bern: Huber, 2008

The Japanese Cult of Tranquility
London: Rider, 1960

Kultur der Stille
Frankfurt/M: Weltz Verlag, 1997

Erikson, Erik H.

Childhood and Society
New York: Norton, 1993
First published in 1950

Ghiselin, Brewster (Ed.)

The Creative Process
Reflections on Invention in the Arts and Sciences
Berkeley: University of California Press, 1985
First published in 1952

Greene, Liz
Astrology of Fate
York Beach, ME: Red Wheel/Weiser, 1986

Saturn
A New Look at an Old Devil
York Beach, ME: Red Wheel/Weiser, 1976

The Astrological Neptune and the Quest for Redemption
Boston: Red Wheel Weiser, 1996

The Mythic Journey
With Juliet Sharman–Burke
The Meaning of Myth as a Guide for Life
New York: Simon & Schuster (Fireside), 2000

Die Mythische Reise
Die Bedeutung der Mythen als ein Führer durch das Leben
München: Atmosphären Verlag, 2004

The Mythic Tarot
With Juliet Sharman–Burke
New York: Simon & Schuster (Fireside), 2001
Originally published in 1986

Le Tarot Mythique
Une nouvelle approche du Tarot
Paris: Solar, 1988

The Luminaries
The Psychology of the Sun and Moon in the Horoscope
With Howard Sasportas
York Beach, ME: Red Wheel/Weiser, 1992

Sonne und Mond
Die Bedeutung der grossen Lichter in der Mythologie und im Horoskop
Saarbrücken: Neue Erde/Lentz, 2000

Hameroff, Newberg, Woolf, Bierman et al.
Consciousness
20 Scientists Interviewed
Director: Gregory Alsbury
5 DVD Box Set, 540 min.
New York: Alsbury Films, 2003

Hicks, Esther and Jerry
The Amazing Power of Deliberate Intent
Living the Art of Allowing
Carlsbad, CA: Hay House, 2006

Houston, Jean
The Possible Human
A Course in Enhancing Your Physical, Mental, and Creative Abilities
New York: Jeremy P. Tarcher/Putnam, 1982

Koestler, Arthur
The Act of Creation
New York: Penguin Arkana, 1989.
Originally published in 1964

Krishnamurti, J.
Education and the Significance of Life
London: Victor Gollancz, 1978

Laszlo, Ervin
Science and the Akashic Field
An Integral Theory of Everything
Rochester: Inner Traditions, 2004

Macroshift
Die Herausforderung
Frankfurt/M: Insel Verlag, 2003

Quantum Shift to the Global Brain
How the New Scientific Reality Can Change Us and Our World
Rochester: Inner Traditions, 2008

Science and the Reenchantment of the Cosmos
The Rise of the Integral Vision of Reality
Rochester: Inner Traditions, 2006

The Akashic Experience
Science and the Cosmic Memory Field
Rochester: Inner Traditions, 2009

The Chaos Point
The World at the Crossroads
Newburyport, MA: Hampton Roads Publishing, 2006

Leonard, George, Murphy, Michael

The Live We Are Given
A Long Term Program for Realizing the
Potential of Body, Mind, Heart and Soul
New York: Jeremy P. Tarcher/Putnam, 1984

Maisel, Eric

Fearless Creating
A Step-By-Step Guide to Starting and Completing
Work of Art
New York: Tarcher & Putnam, 1995

McNiff, Shaun

Art as Medicine
Boston: Shambhala, 1992

Art as Therapy
Creating a Therapy of the Imagination
Boston/London: Shambhala, 1992

Trust the Process
An Artist's Guide to Letting Go
New York: Shambhala Publications, 1998

Meadows, Donella H.

Thinking in Systems
A Primer
White River, VT: Chelsea Green Publishing, 2008

Montessori, Maria

The Absorbent Mind
Reprint Edition
New York: Buccaneer Books, 1995
First published in 1973

Das Kreative Kind
Der absorbierende Geist
Freiburg: Herder, 2007

Murphy, Joseph

The Power of Your Subconscious Mind
West Nyack, N.Y.: Parker, 1981, N.Y.: Bantam, 1982
Originally published in 1962

Die Macht Ihres Unterbewusstseins
München: Hugendubel, 2000

La puissance de votre subconscient
Genève: Ramón Keller, 1967

The Miracle of Mind Dynamics
New York: Prentice Hall, 1964

Miracle Power for Infinite Riches
West Nyack, N.Y.: Parker, 1972

The Amazing Laws of Cosmic Mind Power
West Nyack, N.Y.: Parker, 1973

Secrets of the I Ching
West Nyack, N.Y.: Parker, 1970

Think Yourself Rich
Use the Power of Your Subconscious Mind to Find True Wealth
Revised by Ian D. McMahan, Ph.D.
Paramus, NJ: Reward Books, 2001

Wahrheiten die ihr Leben verändern
Dr. Joseph Murphys Vermächtnis
München: Hugendubel, 1996

Murphy, Michael

The Future of the Body
Explorations into the Further Evolution of Human Nature
New York: Jeremy P. Tarcher/Putnam, 1992

Der Quanten-Mensch
München: Ludwig Verlag, 1996

Myers, Tony Pearce

The Soul of Creativity
Insights into the Creative Process
Novato, CA: New World Library, 1999

Myss, Caroline

The Creation of Health
The Emotional, Psychological, and Spiritual Responses that Promote
Health and Healing
New York: Three Rivers Press, 1998

Naparstek, Belleruth

Your Sixth Sense
Unlocking the Power of Your Intuition
London: HarperCollins, 1998

Ostrander, Sheila & Schroeder, Lynn

Superlearning 2000
New York: Delacorte Press, 1994

Superlearning
Die revolutionäre Lernmethode
München: Scherz Verlag, 1979

Supermemory
New York: Carroll & Graf, 1991

SuperMemory
Der Weg zum optimalen Gedächtnis
München: Goldmann, 1996

Pearce Myers, Tony (Editor)

The Soul of Creativity
Insights into the Creative Process
Novato: New World Library, 1999

Porteous, Hedy S.

Sex and Identity
Your Child's Sexuality
Indianapolis: Bobbs-Merrill, 1972

Radin, Dean

The Conscious Universe
The Scientific Truth of Psychic Phenomena
San Francisco: Harper & Row, 1997

Entangled Minds
Extrasensory Experiences in a Quantum Reality
New York: Paraview Pocket Books, 2006

Rank, Otto

Art and Artist
With Charles Francis Atkinson and Anaïs Nin
New York: W.W. Norton, 1989
Originally published in 1932

Redfield, James

The Tenth Insight
Holding the Vision
New York: Warner Books, 1996

The Celestine Prophecy
New York: Warner Books, 1995

Die Vision von Celestine
Berlin: Ullstein, 2004

Robbins, Anthony

Awaken The Giant Within
New York: Simon & Schuster, 1991

Unlimited Power
The New Science of Personal Achievement
New York: Free Press, 1997

Roberts, Jane

The Nature of Personal Reality
New York: Amber-Allen Publishing, 1994
First published in 1974

Die Natur der Persönlichen Realität
Ein neues Bewusstsein als Quelle der Kreativität
München: Kailash Verlag, 2007

The Nature of the Psyche
Its Human Expression
New York, Amber-Allen Publishing, 1996
First published in 1979

Die Natur der Psyche
Ihr menschlicher Ausdruck in Kreativität, Liebe, Sexualität
Genf: Ariston Verlag, 1985

Die Natur der Psyche
Ihr menschlicher Ausdruck in Kreativität, Liebe, Sexualität
München: Kailash Verlag, 2008

Roman, Sanaya
Opening to Channel
How To Connect With Your Guide
New York: H.J. Kramer, 1987

Zum Höheren Selbst Erwachen
Das Herz dem Bewusstsein des Lichts öffnen
Genf: Ansata Verlag, 2003

Rudhyar, Dane
Astrology of Personality
A Reformulation of Astrological Concepts and Ideals in
Terms of Contemporary Psychology and Philosophy
New York: Aurora Press, 1990

An Astrological Triptych
Gifts of the Spirit, The Way Through, and The Illumined Road
New York: Aurora Press, 1991

Astrological Mandala
New York: Vintage Books, 1994

L'astrologie de la transformation
Paris: Rocher, 1984

Satinover, Jeffrey
The Quantum Brain
New York: Wiley & Sons, 2001

Sher, Barbara & Gottlieb, Annie

Wishcraft
How to Get What You Really Want
2nd edition
New York: Ballantine Books, 2003

Shone, Ronald

Creative Visualization
Using Imagery and Imagination for Self-Transformation
New York: Destiny Books, 1998

Spretnak, Charlene

Green Politics
Rochester, VT: Inner Traditions, 1986

Stein, Robert M.

Redeeming the Inner Child in Marriage and Therapy
in: Reclaiming the Inner Child
ed. by Jeremiah Abrams
New York: Tarcher/Putnam, 1990, 261 ff.

Steiner, Rudolf

Theosophy
An Introduction to the Spiritual Processes in Human Life
and in the Cosmos
New York: Anthroposophic Press, 1994

Die Erziehung des Kindes
Dornach: Rudolf Steiner Verlag, 2003
First published in 1907

Stone, Hal & Stone, Sidra

Embracing Our Selves
The Voice Dialogue Manual
San Rafael, CA: New World Library, 1989

Du bist viele
Das 100fache Selbst und seine Entdeckung durch
die Voice-Dialogue Methode
München: Heyne Verlag, 1994

Whitfield, Charles L.

Healing the Child Within
Deerfield Beach, Fl: Health Communications, 1987Wolf, Fred Alan
Taking the Quantum Leap
The New Physics for Nonscientists
New York: Harper & Row, 1989

Der Quantensprung ist keine Hexerei
Frankfurt/M: Fischer Verlag, 1990

Parallel Universes
New York: Simon & Schuster, 1990

The Dreaming Universe
A Mind-Expanding Journey into the Realm Where
Psyche and Physics Meet
New York: Touchstone, 1995

The Eagle's Quest
A Physicist Finds the Scientific Truth At the Heart of the
Shamanic World
New York: Touchstone, 1997

Die Physik der Träume
Frankfurt/M: DTV Verlag, 1997

Mind into Matter
A New Alchemy of Science and Spirit
New York: Moment Point Press, 2000

Zukav, Gary

The Dancing Wu Li Masters
An Overview of the New Physics
New York: HarperOne, 2001

I've never seen a worse situation than that of young writers in the United States. The publishing business in North America is so commercialized.

– Manuel Puig

FROM THE SAME AUTHOR

A Bibliography

You can search publications from here:
http://ipublica.com/books/

For audio books and music, you can start here:
http://ipublica.com/audio/

All paperbacks, audio downloads, audio book compact discs, music downloads and music compact discs, as well as Kindle books, are referenced on the site.

For free podcasts search iTunes under my author name.

For quoting my publications, please use the following form:
Pierre F. Walter, [Title]: [Subtitle], Newark: Sirius-C Media Galaxy LLC, 2011

Web Presence

Pierre F. Walter on the Web

Sites

http://authoryourlife.com

http://ipublica.com

http://ipublica.net

http://ipublica.org

http://ipublica.tv

Video Channels

http://youtube.com/user/ipublica

http://youtube.com/user/authoryourlife

http://vimeo.com/pierrefwalter/channels

http://ipublica.blip.tv/

http://authoryourlife.blip.tv/

http://emosexuality.blip.tv/

http://pierrefwalter.blip.tv/